T0279092

A STUDIO PRESS BOOK

First published in the UK in 2023 by Studio Press,
an imprint of Bonnier Books UK,
4th Floor, Victoria House, Bloomsbury Square,
London WC1B 4DA
Owned by Bonnier Books, Sveavägen 56, Stockholm, Sweden

www.bonnierbooks.co.uk

1 3 5 7 9 10 8 6 4 2

ISBN 978-1-80078-716-2

Written by Jessica Bumpus
Edited by Stephanie Milton
Designed by Alessandro Susin
Picture Research by Paul Ashman
Production by Emma Kidd

A CIP catalogue record for this book
is available from the British Library

Printed and bound in China

The publisher would like to thank the following for supplying photos for
this book: Alamy, Getty and Shutterstock. Every effort has been made to
obtain permission to reproduce copyright material but there may be cases
where we have not been able to trace a copyright holder. The publisher will
be happy to correct any omissions in future printing.

Vivienne Westwood

The Story Behind the Style

JESSICA BUMPUS

Contents

A Revolutionary Is Born   **6**
Derbyshire Days   **10**
London   **12**
Malcolm McLaren   **16**
Punk   **20**
430 King's Road   **24**
Let It Rock   26
Too Fast to Live, Too Young to Die   28
Sex   30
Seditionaries   32
Worlds End   34
Expansion Part One   **36**
The Orb   **38**
Andreas Kronthaler   **40**
Iconic Collections   **44**
Pirates   48
Nostalgia of Mud/Buffalo   52
Mini-Crini Collection   54
Harris Tweed   56
The Pagan Years   58
Heritage and House Motifs   **60**
Tartan   61
Harris Tweed   62
DIY and Customisation   63
Fashion History and Pearls   64
Corsets and Underwear as Outerwear   65
Political T-shirts   66
Rule-breaking Shoes   68
The Yasmine Bag   72
The "Designer's Designer"   **74**
Brand Overview   **76**
Gold Label   78
Red Label   80
MAN   82

LEFT: Sid Vicious with Vivienne Westwood at a Sex Pistols gig.

Anglomania	84
Andreas Kronthaler for Vivienne Westwood	86
Muse, Sara Stockbridge	**88**
Supermodel Moments	**90**
Naomi Campbell's Platforms	92
Kate Moss' Accessories	94
Pamela Anderson	96
Expansion Part Two	**98**
Fragrance	**100**
Victoria & Albert Museum Exhibition	**102**
Awards and Accolades	**106**
Receiving Her OBE	**108**
Here Comes the Bride	**110**
Sex and the City	**114**
On the Red Carpet	**118**
Campaigns	**120**
RIP 40 Years of Punk	**122**
Documenting Westwood	**124**
Climate Activism	**128**
Protest	**134**
Vivienne Westwood x Burberry	**138**
The TikTok Necklace Phenomenon	**140**
The Last Show	**142**
A Punk Pioneer	**144**
LFW Memorial Service	**146**
Tintwhistle	**148**
A Lasting Legacy	**152**
Image Credits	**156**

A Revolutionary is Born

There are few British designers, or brands, that have made quite as much of an impact on the fashion landscape as Vivienne Westwood. A fashion designer of both cult and commercial success (which is a rare combination), she was a punk and a pioneer, a rebel and a provocateur, an activist and a change-maker.

Over the course of a career that spanned half a century, Dame Vivienne Westwood would become synonymous with the British punk scene. Punk is what immediately springs to mind for most when her name is mentioned, along with the King's Road, corsets, platforms, tartan, crinolines, pirate boots, sustainability and climate change awareness. The list goes on. Her shows and interviews have become legendary – she is famous for using fashion as a platform to speak out on the issues she cared most about.

There is no doubt that Westwood's affinity for fashion history has helped her designs stand out. They are often historically informed, yet never to the point that they look odd. Where something shouldn't work, it always did, thanks to Vivienne's ability to balance the old with the modern – she was a genius when it came to style mashups. And the original Vivienne Westwood aesthetic rooted in a DIY approach never fully went away. Her designs feel intrinsically British and perfectly eccentric.

Westwood was the original multi-hyphenate and, in many ways, light years ahead of her time. She has inspired generations of designers that came after her, whether established and successful or aspiring and eager. Fashion critics even noted whiffs of her spirit at the London Fashion Week collections of autumn/winter 2023, which took place in February 2023, after her death. It's no wonder that her name is up there with the likes of Yves Saint Laurent, Christian Lacroix and the late great Karl Lagerfeld.

ABOVE: Vivienne Westwood takes her bow at the spring/summer 2018 London Fashion Week Men's collections, June 2017.

Her own fashion story is a tale of two halves: pre- and post-the Malcolm McLaren years. The future manager of the Sex Pistols, Malcolm was Vivienne's creative collaborator, and for a time they were in a relationship. It was with Malcolm that she opened the legendary 430 King's Road boutique. It is still there today, known as Worlds End, with a huge clock face upon its whimsical facade. She married Andreas Kronthaler in 1993, with whom she would also creatively collaborate until her death in December 2022.

Vivienne spearheaded moments that became movements, and what started out as motifs of punk, protest and rebellion matured into a fight for sustainability and a fashion life much celebrated.

OPPOSITE: Vivienne Westwood outside Bow Street Magistrate's Court in the late 1970s.

LEFT: Vivienne Westwood poses for a photo in London 1987.

Derbyshire Days

Vivienne Isabel Swire was born on April 8 1941 to Gordon and Dora Swire at the Partington Maternity Home, Glossop. The future fashion revolutionary had one sister, Olga Swire, born 1944, and one brother, Gordon Swire, 1946. She grew up in the parish of Tintwistle, Derbyshire (which was formerly part of Cheshire until 1974), both during and after World War II, enjoying what has been recounted as a fairly idyllic childhood, living at the stone-constructed Millbrook Cottages and playing outside until late.

The young Swire clan were encouraged to be creative and make things more than they were encouraged to read. Vivienne knew from a young age that she was good at making things, notably models at school, and she especially enjoyed sewing classes. Her mother would often make their clothes, and worked as a weaver in a local cotton factory.

The young Vivienne – who remembers having a passionate spirit from an early age – attended Hollingworth and Tintwistle Primary Schools from 1946 to 1952, at which point she passed the scholarship exam for Glossop Grammar School. She continued to be good at art during her time at Glossop Grammar, and considered attending art school.

Among Westwood's noted formative fashion memories are the make-do-and-mend philosophy that came to define

Britain in austerity, as well as the coronation of Queen Elizabeth II in 1953, when Vivienne was 12 years old. The influences of these two events can be seen throughout every era of her designs, and the make-do-and-mend philosophy is evident in the mantra "Buy Less, Choose Well, Make it Last", which the brand still promotes to this day. She expertly blended the elements of customisation, tradition and aristocracy together to create her own unique brand, which is now continued by her husband Andreas Kronthaler.

LEFT: Vivienne Westwood speaking at a festival wearing a "Buy Less" slogan T-shirt.

London

It was in 1957 that a teenage Vivienne Swire moved to London with her family. Her parents believed they would have a better life there, and bought a post office in Harrow. Westwood applied to Harrow Art School, where she was given a place on a jewellery and silversmith course. She would only last a term, however. She quickly grew bored of her course, and she wasn't particularly enamoured, in that moment, with her life in London. She preferred the spontaneity of Manchester, and throughout her life she never lost her distinctive Northern accent. Her time on the jewellery and silversmith course did make her realise what it was that she really wanted to do: make her own clothes. In a memoir about her life, written with the help of the actor and writer Ian Kelly, Vivienne described her own style at the time to be that of a "Trad", or an artist in full skirts and sloppy jumpers.

OPPOSITE: Bustling London: Piccadilly Circus in the West End of London, England.

Soon, the allure of London began to fall into place for Vivienne and she started to form friendships. It was all mods and museums, and she managed to recreate a sense of Manchester's going-out scene. Thinking she wouldn't be able to make a living as an artist, she learned to become a shorthand typist, though she soon discovered that was not what she wanted to do, either. At the age of 19, she attended teacher training college and went on to work at a primary school.

In 1961, she met her first husband, Derek, from whom she would take the Westwood surname. The story goes that they met on the dancefloor; he was an apprentice toolmaker with dreams of becoming a pilot and at the time, he was working for a company that ran dance halls and pop groups. They were married on July 21 1962 at St John the Baptist, Greenhill, and Westwood made her own wedding dress. They welcomed a son, Ben Westwood, in 1963. Not long after – that same year, in fact – Westwood announced she was leaving Derek. They officially split in 1965, setting the stage for a new chapter in Vivienne's life to begin.

OPPOSITE: Piccadilly Circus, London, 1960.

Malcolm McLaren

Westwood met Malcolm McLaren in 1965. An art student and a friend of her younger brother, Gordon, he would go on to become her creative collaborator for almost the next 20 years. Malcolm is as synonymous with the punk movement as Vivienne, and their partnership is legendary. He was something of a mastermind of marketing anarchy and disruption, before such things became commonplace in contemporary fashion. The pair were in a relationship for a time but never seem to have married.

Malcolm was interested in politics and was fascinated by the French Situationists, a creative enclave of writers and artists who wished to eradicate capitalism through acts of everyday life. He was a driving force in bringing politics, provocation, society and culture into Westwood's world. She found him to be charismatic and knowledgeable, but also full of contradictions.

In 1967, they had a son, Joseph Ferdinand Corré, who would go on to follow in his parents' footsteps and enter the world of fashion. He founded the very successful lingerie company, Agent Provocateur.

It was in the early 1970s that McLaren and Westwood began to build their empire. Malcolm, by this point, had left art school and Vivienne was about to quit teaching. The plan had been to sell vintage records together, and there was talk of setting up a stall. But a retail opportunity – via a new friend – on King's Road was about to arise.

Tommy Roberts, of the legendary Mr Freedom fashion business, took over the lease of 430 King's Road in 1969. He and his business partner, the fashion entrepreneur Trevor Myles, were well-known for their eclectic and discerning fashion eye which appealed to the gliteratti of the 1960s. It was under Myles' control the shop was renamed Paradise Garage; the spot was already well-known for fashion.

Vivienne and Malcolm, who were regulars on King's Road, ended up renting the back of 430 King's Road, before taking the whole thing over and rebranding it. It would be known over the coming years as Let It Rock, Too Fast To Live, Too Young To Die and Sex and Seditonaries, all of which would encompass the nuanced, confrontational and non-conformist nature of McLaren and Westwood. Eventually the shop would come to define the varied-but-defined styles we know as punk today.

LEFT: Malcolm McLaren, manager of Sex Pistols, and Vivienne Westwood, 1977.

LEFT: Malcolm
McLaren, who was
Westwood's longtime
collaborator.

OPPOSITE: Westwood
and McLaren inside
their shop on the King's
Road, circa 1985.

Politics and anti-capitalist ideology were not McLaren's only passions – he was also passionate about music. For a time he would manage and dress the US band the New York Dolls, who are linked to the birth of the American punk scene. He then returned to London where, operating from King's Road's Sex, as it was then named, he would become the manager of The Sex Pistols, arbiters of punk from 1975 until their demise in 1978.

Consisting of band members Johnny Rotten, Paul Cook, Steve Jones, Glen Matlock and later Sid Vicious, Sex Pistols were well-known for their raucous and anti-establishment songs like 'Anarchy in the UK', accompanied by equally raucous and anti-establishment behaviour. The band performed its 'God Save the Queen' anthem – a song often banned from being played in respectable establishments – on a boat outside the Houses of Parliament in London. They would wear Westwood and

McLaren's designs, inextricably linking the messages of their music with Malcolm and Vivienne's riotous-looking designs.

McLaren died in 2010 at the age of 64. He was remembered for his publicity stunts, and involvement with culture and music. While the relationship between him and Vivienne might have formally ended during the 1980s, in her memoir she acknowledges his significant influence on her, what they achieved, the trouble they got into and his role in their pioneering and creative partnership. Westwood's obituaries also noted her grace and generosity about him.

Punk

Punk emerged during the mid-1970s. It was a music and fashion phenomenon with geographic roots in both London and New York, specifically the King's Road (during the 1960s it had been home to another shake-up style scene: London's Swinging Sixties, the Youthquake) and the East Village. It also had ideological roots in alienation and anti-establishment. It is described as being a city-centric style movement: both a look and a music genre, but also an attitude, a way of acting and anarchy. In fashion terms, it is broadly viewed as being defined by leather jackets, chains, studs, safety pins, string vests, spiked hair and an aura of intimidation – visual signifiers of rebellion and disturbing the peace.

In various forms, these styles had already been adopted by American bands at this time, including The Ramones and the New York Dolls, the latter of whom had visited Westwood and McLaren in their shop.

In 1973, McLaren and Westwood went to the US. It was Westwood's first time in the country, and it was a visit that proved to have quite an impact. Where McLaren was inspired by the music scene, Vivienne was inspired by the influential characters she met, who were already leaning into the styles they had been cultivating back at 430 King's Road. Westwood and McLaren had been customising T-shirts in what could certainly be deemed as punk style. And the whole enterprise of their business, which wasn't exactly traditional or typical, was also pretty punk from the outset.

While McLaren managed the New York Dolls, then put together Sex Pistols, Westwood had her own punk epiphany: and the resulting designs were keenly embraced by the Pistols' Johnny Rotten (though it is claimed that he was the instigator of safety pins in fashion) as well as by the rest of the band. Punk, therefore, was a collision of these forces: Westwood, McLaren, Sex Pistols and King's Road – with a splash of New York.

BELOW: Poster boy of punk, Johnny Rotten of Sex Pistols, circa 1976.

OVERLEAF LEFT: A policeman arresting a punk in Sloane Square, Chelsea, 1977.

OVERLEAF RIGHT: Pamela Rooke and Simon Barker in 'God Save the Queen' T shirts.

430 King's Road

K ing's Road, Chelsea, is an address now legendary for its affiliation with fashion. Before Westwood and McLaren, there was Mary Quant, but it's Westwood and McLaren's 430 King's Road in particular which draws crowds of people pursuing a fashion-history pilgrimage, even to this day. It was a fashion youth mecca and the headquarters from which Vivienne Westwood and Malcolm McLaren masterminded collections that would shape, shift and subvert London's style scene for decades to come. She took care of the clothes, he took care of the interiors.

Having gone through various incarnations over the years, today the shop is known as Worlds End. You'll find it just beyond the bend in the road at Milman's Street and Park Walk – a charming blue exterior that looks ever so slightly like something you'd come across in a theme park. It is also located at what is known as Worlds End bus stop. Westwood and McLaren first opened the store in 1971 (it was formerly a pawnbroker's, a grocer's and downstairs, a restaurant), and renamed it according to each new collection that followed.

Today, fashion operates seasonally to a six-month cycle, with autumn/winter and spring/summer collections revealed at the beginning and end of the year. At the Worlds End HQ, it was more about a feeling; collections would move on when Westwood and McLaren felt it was time and they would rename the shop accordingly, breaking all the rules to create their own way of life.

ABOVE: A punk helps a passer-by on King's Road, Chelsea, during the 1970s.

Let It Rock

When it first opened in 1971, the King's Road boutique was known as Let It Rock. Initially, Westwood and McLaren had been interested in 1950s clothing, records and memorabilia – a time period that went against the grain of the hippy moment that was prevalent in the 70s. They would go down to Brick Lane or Brixton Market and pick up all manner of 50s clothes to rework and sell on, such as Teddy Boy suits (already a staple of McLaren's style), brothel creepers and stilettos, as well as various ephemera. The shop became part installation, part brand-new retail experience. Soon, everyone wanted to go there and be seen there. It was considered the epicentre of youth culture.

LEFT: A group of Teddy Boys dancing at the London rock 'n' roll revival show in Wembley Arena, 1972. Initially, McLaren and Westwood had been inspired by the 1950s and Teddy Boys.

OPPOSITE: Wearing pieces from SW3's coolest shops, Mr Freedom and Let It Rock, which is where the motorcyclist's gear is from, 1973.

Too Fast to Live, Too Young to Die

About a year later, the store was renamed Too Fast To Live, Too Young To Die, or TFTLTYTD as it was commonly abbreviated. The new look that it ushered in was equally provocative. Inspired by rockers and Hells Angels, it focused on customised T-shirts printed with graphics and slogans, featuring chains, studs, black leather, badges – in one instance, boiled chicken bones spelled out "Rock" to create a piece which has become an iconic early design of the duo. It was around this time that the roots of punk were starting to spread.

OPPOSITE: American rock band New York Dolls, 1973.

ABOVE: New York Punk Club CBGB, founded by Hilly Kristal in 1973.

Sex

By 1974 the store was renamed Sex and the outside of the building said so in giant pink rubberised letters. At the time, perhaps more seedy Soho than chichi Chelsea, the clothes featured rips, cuts and holes, torn hems and seams outside, and explored the kinkier side of life with spike stilettos and other deliberate shock-factor ideas.

Famously, the musician Chrissie Hynde was a shop assistant at Sex, as was Pamela Rooke, otherwise known as Jordan. She was well-known for commuting up each day from Sussex, where she was upgraded to First Class because passengers kept complaining about her clothes – or lack of them. Her uniform of choice was a net top, rubber skirt and stilettos. Intimidating, confident and glamorous, she was arguably one of the early faces or ambassadors of Westwood style. There would, of course, be others.

LEFT: Pamela Rooke, aka Jordan, inside Sex, 1976.

OPPOSITE: Pamela Rooke outside Sex in 1976.

Seditionaries

The shop's next incarnation was Seditionaries in 1976. During this punk phase, Westwood explored straps and zips, bondage and fetishism themes and transformed them into a new type of fashion. The riskiness and deviance of the Sex days were still evident, but added to that was combat gear, motorcyclists' leathers, unravelling mohair sweaters, torn-looking dresses, metal chains and safety pins, giving a distressed and deconstructed nature to the clothes. Graphics were confrontational and cheeky. The band Sex Pistols pertinently wore various items from the Seditionaries era.

ABOVE: Seditionaries styles featured chains and tartan with a biker flourish.

OPPOSITE: Punk fashion from Seditionaries, modelled by Simon and Jordan, 1977.

Worlds End

In 1979, the store changed once more, to Worlds End (partly, it's thought, in reference to the location of the shop which is much further down King's Road than one might think). The shop retains the Worlds End livery today, its 13-hour clock ticking backwards atop its striking galleon-esque exterior. Most recently, it became a place of mourning; flowers and tributes were poignantly laid outside the quirky little shop following the death of its founder, in December 2022.

Westwood and McLaren would end their relationship in 1981, but they continued with their business partnership for a while longer. A second shop, Nostalgia of Mud, would open in 1982 in St Christopher's Place, W1. But the future of Vivienne Westwood lay overseas, and she would soon relocate to Italy. There would be a bit of a detour via potential deals and expansion before Worlds End reopened again in 1986, this time without McLaren.

OPPOSITE: Models wearing Westwood outside Worlds End, circa 1980s.

RIGHT: Worlds End, the legendary shop where it all began, in Chelsea.

Expansion Part One

Following McLaren and Westwood's wave-making run in fashion, Worlds End closed for a time in the early to mid 1980s (accounts vary) and the punk duo went their separate creative ways. Westwood met business manager Carlo D'Amario around 1982, and there was talk of him doing PR for her. But what transpired was a potential deal with Fiorucci, the Italian fashion brand with whom he worked, to produce clothes in Italy. At the time, designs sold in the Worlds End store featured a Worlds End label – they weren't branded Vivienne Westwood, and this was something D'Amario was keen to address. Here, accounts get a little foggy: there seems to have been a potential licensing agreement with Giorgio Armani in 1984 which, to followers of fashion, might seem like something of an unlikely pairing. But no clothes were ever produced.

In 1986, D'Amario was appointed managing director of Vivienne Westwood and, that same year, she returned to London from Italy. The next phase of Westwood's career was about to begin – it would be a move towards fitted silhouettes, tailoring and a deep dive into the history of fashion which would inform designs that would cement her signature style for the next 40 years. As a result, another round of expansion would occur – this time globally. The Vivienne Westwood brand was starting to emerge.

OPPOSITE: Inside a Vivienne Westwood store in Los Angeles, California, 2011.

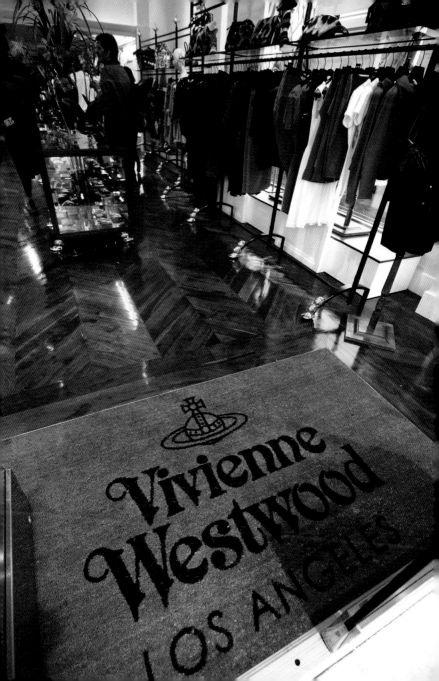

The Orb

A side from the tartan, the platforms and the pearls (and countless other symbols Westwood has made her own), there is one particular motif that is perhaps more synonymous with the brand than the rest, certainly in marketing terms: the Vivienne Westwood orb logo.

The orb came later in her career, post the Malcolm McLaren years. They formally ended their collaboration in 1984, and Westwood needed to work out who and what she was by herself, so that she could begin to shape the future of her brand. The days of punk, DIY and anarchy were largely behind her, though elements of them would always find their way in to her creations.

The orb logo debuted around 1986. Following a hiatus during which the Worlds End shop was closed, Westwood, now in Italy, was working on a collection inspired by royalty but with a futuristic nod. It was while she was envisaging a jumper that Prince Charles might wear that the royal insignia, particularly the orb, came into play. She added a satellite ring around it, as the required nod to the future. At the time, Carlo D'Amario, her business manager, said it would be the ideal logo for her brand. It has since featured on everything from bags to T-shirts, buttons to fragrance bottles. It perfectly encapsulates that sense of tradition, force and vision that the brand is known for.

At the time, though, Westwood encountered a slight hiccup. The orb logo was very similar to Harris Tweed's logo. It is an issue that, according to the clothmaker, has since been resolved. Westwood has often used the cloth in her collections and expressed a love for doing so. There would even be a collection named Harris Tweed.

OPPOSITE: The Vivienne
Westwood orb logo.

Andreas Kronthaler

Following her split from Malcolm McLaren – the man she credited with helping her to discover society, politics and culture – and a hiatus from London and the King's Road, Vivienne Westwood entered a new phase in her life and career. While teaching in the late 1980s in Vienna (she was appointed Professor of Fashion at the Vienna Academy of Applied Arts from 1989 to 1991) she met Austrian Andreas Kronthaler, then a student.

Born in 1966, Kronthaler was brought up in rural Tyrol. Aged 19, he enrolled at the Vienna Academy of Applied Arts to study industrial design, but reapplied three years later to study fashion under Westwood. Kronthaler was 23 and Westwood was 48, and the 25-year age gap has sometimes invited comment.

Right from the start, Westwood and Kronthaler had a mutual respect and intrigue for one another. They went on to collaborate; she said he introduced her to the possibilities of couture and how it could impact her designs. They would go on to be partners in life and work over the coming decades; she found herself able to bounce ideas off him and he, in turn, enjoyed offering his design references for inspiration. They married in 1993 and together envisaged another new direction for the brand that would take the 1990s by storm. For the War & Peace collection of spring/summer 2012, she brought Kronthaler out with her for the first time at the show's finale.

Kronthaler would eventually take over what was known as the Gold Label range – it became known as Andreas Kronthaler for Vivienne Westwood for the autumn/winter 2016-17 season. Westwood would continue to design the main Vivienne Westwood line, which covered all the other ranges under one umbrella label.

Kronthaler's second collection for Andreas Kronthaler for Vivienne Westwood was Europa for spring/summer 2017, designed in dedication to the continent of Europe following Brexit.

Increasingly, his collections would become more personal and reflect his own heritage, which included his relationship with Vivienne.

PREVIOUS: Vivienne Westwood accompanied by her husband Andreas Kronthaler, arriving for a reception at No. 10 Downing Street, 1997.

OPPOSITE: Westwood with Andreas Kronthaler at the autumn/winter 1995 show in Paris.

Iconic Collections

I n the wake of her death, Westwood has been described as an iconoclast, a maverick and a creative genius; the influence she has had on fashion is global, and undeniable. When one thinks of Westwood they think of so many things – all of which feel inherently Westwood. And beyond those first collections born from Worlds End – Let It Rock, Too Fast to Live, Too Young to Die, Sex – there have been plenty more that stand out as definitive moments in both her career and fashion generally. Of course, any Westwood fan will have their own personal highlights. But one moment that stands out for most is her catwalk debut, Pirates, in 1981.

OPPOSITE: Model Naomi Campbell and Westwood attend the Designer of the Year Awards at the Natural History Museum, 1993.

RIGHT: Supermodel Linda Evangelista modelling at the Vivienne Westwood autumn/winter 1995 show in Paris.

OVERLEAF: Finishing touches, backstage at an autumn/winter 1991-92 show.

an exhibition about arthropods

Pirates

The Pirate collection, sometimes known as Pirates, was the first collection shown on the London catwalk. Held at Pillar Hall in Olympia in 1981, it was the autumn/winter 1981-82 season. Worlds End had been decorated to match it, as a pirate ship, or galleon, with sloping floors. Westwood was still working with McLaren at this time.

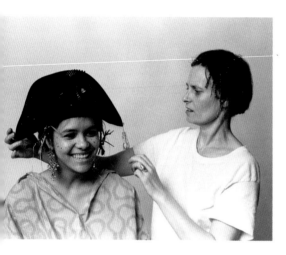

LEFT: Bow Wow Wow lead singer Annabella Lwin with Westwood in London, 1980.

OPPOSITE: From the iconic Pirates 1981 collection.

In this collection, Westwood incorporated historical cuts and explored the concept that they were plundering ideas from other time periods and cultures. There were whiffs of 17th and 18th century garments, with baggy crotch trousers, oversized shirts, sashes and bicorne hats. It's from this show that the graphic squiggle print originated. The bright colours – yellow, red, blue – and romantic feel all went down a treat, and chimed with a new music and fashion era known as the New Romantic movement. International stockists abounded.

Nostalgia of Mud/Buffalo

The autumn/winter 1982-83 collection was titled Nostalgia of Mud and came at the same time as Westwood and McLaren's store of the same name, which operated out of St Christopher's Place in central London. Interestingly, the collection is also sometimes referred to as the Buffalo collection – McLaren had his single Buffalo Gals out at the same time. The collection was seen to be a mix of references, spanning the American Wild West, bras which were worn on the outside, and traditional dress of Andean cultures. It was as a result of this collection that underwear as outerwear started to become a Westwood invention and style.

PREVIOUS LEFT: Pirates was the pair's first catwalk show in 1981.

PREVIOUS RIGHT: Pirates 1981 collection in London.

LEFT: Malcolm McLaren in the Buffalo collection, London, 1983.

RIGHT: Apparently at a Buffalo party, Malcolm McLaren with models wearing pieces from the collection of the same name, London 1983.

Mini-Crini Collection

The spring/summer 1986 collection was the first following Westwood's official split with McLaren, and it marked the debut of the Vivienne Westwood label. It was a gear shift and proved to be as memorable to the designer as it was to fashion fans – she would revisit elements from it throughout the remainder of the decade. It's where corsets are thought to have entered the equation; the idea of underwear as outerwear – one of many concepts credited to her – and where tailoring started to become more apparent.

In true Westwood fashion, it went against the then vogue for futurism and shoulder pads – trends that fellow fashion designers such as Mugler were embracing. Instead, Westwood explored the aesthetics of 19th century crinoline and was inspired by the doll in the ballet *Petrushka*, as well as a photograph of the Queen.

Giant spots, checks and stars featured on splaying skirts and models wore ballet-like shoes built up on wooden blocks which rocked as they walked. These shoes were one of several footwear designs Westwood would be remembered for.

OPPOSITE: Mini-Crini featured shapely but short silhouettes.

LEFT: The iconic Mini-Crini collection for spring/summer 1986.

Harris Tweed

Harris Tweed, the autumn/winter 1987-88 collection, was deemed a comeback for Westwood. It was imbued with royal and aristocratic aesthetics and associations, as well as the heritage cloth she loved to use. It also featured Sadie Frost and Sara Stockbridge modelling. The latter became something of a muse for the house of Westwood – she would walk time and again for the designer throughout the 1980s and 1990s.

LEFT: Malcolm McLaren and Vivienne Westwood, Canada, circa 1987.

OPPOSITE: A look from the Harris Tweed collection, 1987.

The corset featured once again, as did stereotypes of Britishness, with tailoring worn over mini-crinis. Twinsets and pearls, bright punchy colours, and smudged lipstick to suggest the aftermath of kissing. And the master milliner Stephen Jones made spoof crowns to go with the whole wonky, upper-class look.

The Pagan Years

A period that has come to be known as The Pagan Years
ran from the end of the 1980s to the early 1990s, starting
with Britain Must Go Pagan for spring/summer 1988. It
would kickstart a series of collections that explored art and
antiquity alongside English tailoring. Greco-Roman themes
had first been explored by Westwood in Hypnos, 1984, and
she credits her friend Gary Ness as having opened her mind
to a lot of the ideas regarding art and history that would
wind their way into her collections.

Jackets were cropped, dresses soft and corsets featured
drapery to mimic that of statues, while sandals featured
wings. A knee-length bustle-back skirt that featured was
called Centaur and Harris Tweed would once again make an
appearance.

Further collections from this period are often namechecked,
including Witches autumn/winter 1983-84 which saw a
team-up with the artist Keith Haring. This would also be
the last Worlds End collection from McLaren and Westwood
together. Voyage to Cythera, for autumn/winter 1989-
90, saw models in bodysuits with fig leaves positioned
on the necessary areas; Portrait, autumn/winter 1990-91,
was historical and extravagant, full of pearls and heaving
bosoms; Anglomania for autumn/winter 1993-94 will
forever be known for the supermodel Naomi Campbell
taking a tumble from her supremely high platforms; Les
femmes ne connaissent pas toute leur coquetterie for spring/
summer 1996 was dominated by swishing skirts.

More recently, it's those collections that have shone a
torch on the causes most important to the brand that have
garnered attention: Propaganda autumn/winter 2005-6;

Active Resistance spring/summer 2006; Climate Revolution spring/summer 2013. Down to No. 10 spring/summer 2021 marked the 40th anniversary of the designer's catwalk debut, as well as her 50th in fashion, Kronthaler's 30th in fashion and the tenth for the Andreas Kronthaler for Vivienne Westwood label.

LEFT: The Voyage to Cythera collection autumn/winter 1989-90.

Heritage and House Motifs

Whether from the days of Malcolm McLaren or those of Andreas Kronthaler, there is a certain visual language, and series of underlying leitmotifs and hallmarks, that are synonymous with the Vivienne Westwood world. For a designer who has had so many chapters – which from afar can look disparate but in reality share many commonalities – it's quite a feat that all of them still feel so inherently Westwood. Most brands will typically have a handful of signatures, but Westwood has a whole wardrobe.

Tartan

The Scottish patterned cloth has featured in various Westwood collections throughout the years including autumn/winter 1988-89's Time Machine and the iconic autumn/winter 1993 collection, Anglomania. It was for this collection that Westwood created her own tartan, Westwood MacAndreas, which Lochcarron of Scotland, the leading manufacturer of tartan, officially recognises as a clan. To this day, it is still used in Westwood's collections and other tartans have also been introduced, including the MacPoiret, named after the couturier Paul Poiret.

OPPOSITE: Westwood with her muse, Sara Stockbridge, October 1991.

ABOVE: Westwood's designs at London Fashion Week autumn/winter 2014.

Harris Tweed

Westwood designed the Harris Tweed collection for the
autumn/winter 1987 season. This drew attention to the
storied clothmaker, whose production process and resulting
product must adhere to The Act of Parliament 1993: the
cloth must be made from pure virgin wool which has
been dyed and spun on the Outer Hebrides islands and
handwoven at the home of the weaver. It is a highly revered
craft and skill.

The collection also played into a fascination Westwood had
at the time with tradition and the countryside; little jackets,
twinsets and pearls featured in the collection. The cloth has
since reappeared in other collections. Westwood said the
original collection was inspired by a little girl she had seen
on the tube wearing a Harris Tweed jacket.

DIY and Customisation

Westwood was combining fashion, politics and recycling before it was trendy to do so. Brought up in a make-do-and-mend era, DIY and customisation were ingrained in Westwood's DNA, and resulted in the "Buy Less, Choose Well, Make It Last" mantra she adopted in later years.

In the early years of the 430 King's Road shop, customisation was key for Westwood when it came to creating politically-charged style statements. She often used unique and non-conformist means to express herself, such as chicken bones spelling out the word "rock" and sewn onto a T-shirt. Studs, safety pins and slogans followed – she had a knack for taking basic, everyday objects and turning them on their head to make something innovative, cool and beautiful (or obscene, depending on your stance on punk at the time). It was, in that sense, very Situationist.

Later, Westwood would use the catwalk as an impromptu platform to stage her protests and campaigns.

Fashion History and Pearls

One of the most notable things about Vivienne Westwood's designs is that they borrow from the past, but deliver in the now. Even in the very beginning, it was the 1950s that served as a historical reference point and USP for Westwood, when everyone else was looking to the hippy movement. As she became a solo designer and then teamed up with Andreas Kronthaler, her designs started to take a dive into the fashion history archives: swagged and sweeping ball gowns, corsets, crinolines, pearls and tailoring all factored in.

It was during The Pagan Years that there was a deep focus on cultural history, with collection pieces looking as though they could have been plucked from the set of Dangerous Liaisons, or which explored themes from the ancient worlds.

LEFT: Westwood in her Battersea studio.

OPPOSITE: Corsets began to feature in Westwood's collections during the 1980s. Here, taken in 1990, we see two designs which are now instantly recognisable from the Portrait collection.

Corsets and Underwear as Outerwear

The trend for corsets and underwear as outerwear is famously attributed to Westwood – the autumn/winter 1982-83 Nostalgia of Mud collection featured bras worn over the top of hoodies and dresses. Westwood wanted to challenge the notion of why bras are worn, and then add petticoats and "bag" boots to the look. It made a significant impact, and seemed quite avant-garde at the time, when fashion ran to more rigid rules.

Corsets were a Westwood collection feature from the Harris Tweed collection onwards. They would be seen in Britain Must Go Pagan, Time Machine, Portrait, War & Peace and more besides. They came back in fashion once more in the early 2020s thanks to Westwood and her popularity on TikTok.

Political T-shirts

There are a handful of fashion designers who can lay claim to playing an important role in the boom of the political and/or slogan T-shirt, from Katharine Hamnett's "Choose Life" slogan campaign in the 1980s to Henry Holland's House of Holland fashion rhyming slang in the mid 2000s. Westwood, too, is part of this grouping, though her contribution began back in the 1970s.

Her customised and confrontational T-shirts are intrinsic to punk style and started life during 430 King's Road's Let It Rock and Too Fast to Live, Too Young to Die, or TFTLTYTD, phase. McLaren and Westwood customised black T-shirts that had words like "Scum" or "Venus" or "Rock" written across them. Glitter, glue, studs and chains were used to construct these now rare and valuable pieces, whose status-quo-shifting messaging would soon progress from simple slogans to graphics, too. Among the most controversial included the

swastika T-shirt, the "How to make a Molotov cocktail" T-shirt, a T-shirt with two cowboys naked from the waist down, their Sex Pistols T-shirts, the God Save the Queen T-shirt, and the Naked Breast T-shirt. On more than one occasion, their designs, and accompanying antics, got them into trouble with the law.

Westwood never stopped making political statements – social justice issues were always important to her. But over the past 20 years, she had also turned her attention to the environment, climate change and fracking, as well as throwing her support behind figures including Julian Assange. The way she spread her message, in something of a full-circle moment, was via the humble T-shirt.

OPPOSITE: Politics has gone hand in hand with fashion for Westwood. Here, the designer is in Parliament Square, London, to mark the 50th birthday of Julian Assange in July 2021.

Rule-breaking Shoes

Vivienne Westwood was frequently spotted cycling on her bike around London – often in huge heels or giant platforms. Footwear is an important part of the Westwood brand and among its offerings are some very distinct styles. Naturally, platforms – very very high platforms – feature. Westwood has been known to say that height puts a woman's beauty on a pedestal. In 1993, the supermodel Naomi Campbell famously took a tumble on the catwalk wearing a pair of very high platforms – known as the Super Elevated Gillie heels – for the Anglomania collection. This infamous pair in blue mock-croc cemented their status as a Westwood mainstay, not to mention their place in the fashion history books. Apparently, they measure 30.5 cm tall! If you wish to see them in the flesh, they are a part of the Victoria & Albert Museum collection.

"Animal toe" shoes are another Vivienne Westwood classic. Their name sums them up pretty well; introduced in the Summertime spring/summer 2000 collection, it's as though a mythical creature has tried on your shoes, leaving the imprint of their foot in the leather, the outline of the toes clearly visible. They appeared again in spring/summer 2002's Nymph collection and once more in the spring/summer 2020 Rock Me Amadeus collection. They have also been worked into a more practical gym shoe.

Sexy stilettos were also among Westwood and McLaren's arsenal during the days of Sex at 430 King's Road. At the time they offered looks featuring spikes, buckles and PVC, with footwear following in a similar deviant design to the clothes on offer.

There were also sandals and slippers – the latter, once again, extreme. Exploring lofty heights, a Rocking Horse slipper with a 14 cm-tall wooden sole was first introduced with the spring/summer 1985 Mini-Crini collection and, indeed, did rock as one walked. Inspiration is said to have come from clogs worn by Geishas.

TOP: Westwood's Rocking Horse Ballerina shoes, 1986.

LEFT: The mock-croc Elevated Gillies, from which Naomi Campbell famously fell.

OPPOSITE: Pirate boots from Westwood's Pirates autumn/winter 1981 collection.

On the boot front, there are the famous Pirate boots of 1981, and before them the Seditionaries bondage boots of 1976. The former were part of Westwood and McLaren's first catwalk collection for the autumn/winter 1981-82 season, and have become a modern classic. They have famously been worn by Kate Moss and Sienna Miller, who both gave them a more bohemian spin.

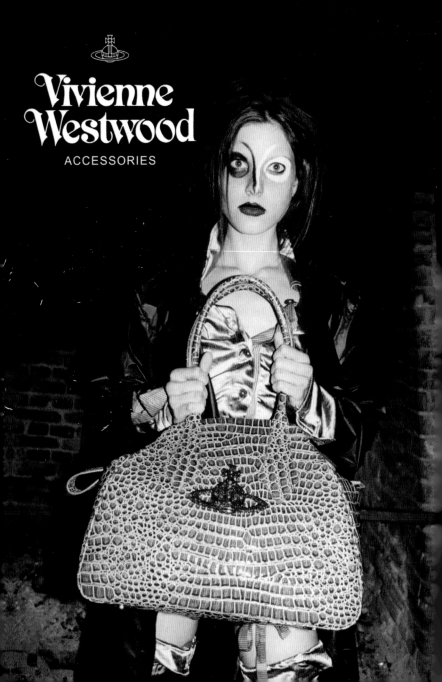

The Yasmine Bag

One of the most important things a designer brand should have is a recognisable bag. And for Vivienne Westwood, that's the Yasmine bag. It was introduced for the autumn/winter 1988 season in a show titled Time Machine. According to the Vivienne Westwood website blog, it was originally named after the French designer Yasmine Eslami, who worked for Westwood during the 1980s; she had the first prototype. It would also be seen at further shows including Café Society in spring/summer 1994 and Anglomania in autumn/winter 1993-94.

OPPOSITE: A magazine advert from the 2010s featuring the Yasmine bag.

ABOVE: Kate Moss with her daughter Lila at the memorial service for Westwood. Lila carries a heart-shaped Westwood bag.

Its shape is practical and feels like a cross between a bowling bag and something more historic – an enlarged coin purse, perhaps. Featuring the orb logo at the top, it has, over the years, gone up and down in size, gone vegan, and been created in a multitude of colours, but always remained recognisable as a Vivienne Westwood piece. In a similar way that the proportions of the brand's shoes and outfit silhouettes are so recognisable, the same can be said for the Yasmine. Other recognisable bags include the Ella and Louise bags, both of which are heart shaped.

The "Designer's Designer"

I t's not just customers that love Westwood, it's designers too. It is well known that John Fairchild – the legendary publisher and editor of the trade title *Women's Wear Daily* – said there would be six designers who would be remembered from the end of the 20th century. Alongside the French fashion designer Yves Saint Laurent, the Italian Giorgio Armani, French Emanuel Ungaro, Chanel designer Karl Lagerfeld and French fashion designer Christian Lacroix was Britain's very own Vivienne Westwood. Interestingly, she was the only woman to be cited among the list.

Fairchild crowned Westwood the "designer's designer", which among the fashion world conveys the idea that the details, references and nuances used are the kind only a fellow designer would catch or appreciate. Today, one could refer to Raf Simons as a designer's designer, or Miuccia Prada (funnily enough, the pair now work together on the Prada line).

OPPOSITE:
A starry designer front row at Paris Fashion Week spring/summer 1994. Left to right: Azzedine Alaïa, Jean Paul Gaultier and John Galliano.

Among the designers that turned out to Westwood's Southwark Cathedral memorial included Paul Smith, Giles Deacon, Matty Bovan and Erdem Moralıoğlu, while tributes came in following the news of her death from across the globe – including Michael Kors, Tommy Hilfiger and Marc Jacobs.

Also of note: in 1983, Westwood received an invitation to show her spring/summer Hypnos collection in Tokyo as part of the Best of Five global fashion awards alongside Calvin Klein, Claude Montana, Hanae Mori and Gianfranco Ferré. She was seen as being right up there with the greats. Her influence on fashion, and the designers who either came up alongside her or after her, has also been politely observed over the years – she is said to have paved the way. She certainly had many supporters.

Brand Overview

When Vivienne Westwood and Malcolm McLaren operated out of 430 King's Road, they were making collections that more or less matched the name or theme of the store at the time. When they were interested in the 1950s, that's what they matched to. When they got bored of that, they moved on, which took them from punk to fetish and more. It wasn't until the Pirates collection in 1981 that they actually showed on a catwalk. Pirates riffled through history and brought with it a new romantic mood. The pirate theme also extended to the interior of Worlds End, which at that time had a galleon feel to it. The collection is one of the most famous and spawned the cult pirate boots.

Westwood and McLaren's partnership ended in 1983 (and formally ended in 1984) She then met Carlo D'Amario, who would be appointed as managing director of Vivienne Westwood in 1986. The same year, Westwood returned to London from Italy and reopened Worlds End. Numerous vibrant and innovative collections – and the arrival of Andreas Kronthaler, her next creative collaborator and later husband – would ensue over the next decade, and the business also became more structured. Cue the Red Label, Gold Label, MAN, and Anglomania lines. There would also be jewellery and perfume licenses.

OPPOSITE: Westwood attends the Vivienne Westwood US flagship store grand opening on March 30, 2011, in Los Angeles, California.

Vivienne Westwood
Vivienne Westwood
Vivienne Westwood
Vivienne Westwood
Vivienne Westwood

Vivienne
Westwood

GOLD LABEL

Gold Label

Following the debut of the Vivienne Westwood brand and roughly a decade's worth of collections, things started to become more streamlined and organised. In 1993, for the Anglomania autumn/winter 1993-94 collection, the Gold Label was introduced. It should not be confused with another line, a diffusion line called Anglomania, which was introduced later.

Gold Label was the catwalk offering, and considered something of a flagship line. It would now be produced in London and to demi-couture standards. Gold Label would become Andreas Kronthaler for Vivienne Westwood in 2016. It was typically shown on the catwalks of Paris Fashion Week twice a year and therefore rightly placed Westwood among fashion's best couturiers.

OPPOSITE: An advert for Gold Label from the 2010s.

RIGHT: Kate Moss in the autumn/ winter 1993 collection in Paris.

Red Label

Westwood's Red Label appeared in the 1990s – some say 1993 and others say 1999, accounts seem to vary. The aim of this line was to be more ready-to-wear focused. It was a diffusion, more readily accessible and aimed at a slightly younger audience, but still with core Westwood styles and ideas.

Over the years, it was often shown during London Fashion Week, where its younger, punkier spirit worked well for the fashion capital and brought with it a host of famous faces both on and off the catwalk. This included everyone from onlookers like Kelly Osbourne, Cuba Gooding Jr and Erin O'Connor to those taking a turn on the runway such as Jaime Winstone, Daisy Lowe, Alice Dellal and even Alexa Chung. On one occasion the model Lily Cole – who is also known for her activism and environmental works – did an interpretive dance.

LEFT: Fellow activist Lily Cole at the Red Label spring/summer 2014 show during Fashion Week.

OPPOSITE: Daisy Lowe on the catwalk at London Fashion Week for the Vivienne Westwood Red Label autumn/winter 2015 show.

MAN

The Vivienne Westwood MAN menswear label debuted in 1996 and would thereafter be shown in Milan each season at the bi-annual menswear shows. Menswear was not brand new to Westwood (and certainly, clothing born at 430 King's Road was largely unisex). Early collections featured both men and women on the catwalk and the designer had held a standalone menswear show as part of the menswear industry showcase Pitti – which takes place in Florence, Italy – in 1990. Titled Cut and Slash, it featured clothes that had, as the name suggested, been cut and slashed open for spring/summer 1991.

But, in January 2017, the brand announced that both Red Label and MAN would now come under one umbrella – Vivienne Westwood – and be shown together. It was part of a new phase of streamlining for the brand which encapsulated its ongoing motto of "Buy Less, Choose Well, Make It Last". The Worlds End Collection, Anglomania diffusion line and the accessory lines continued as they were.

OPPOSITE: Westwood at her spring/summer 2001 menswear show.

LEFT: A Vivienne Westwood design as seen in the Milano Moda Uomo autumn/winter 2010-11 event in Milan, Italy, 2010.

Anglomania

As well as being the name of an earlier collection (the one in which Kate Moss was dressed up as a stunning tartan bride for the finale, and Naomi Campbell tripped in her platform boots, in 1993), Anglomania was a diffusion line introduced in 1998. It takes its style cues from archive Westwood collections, drawing particularly on tailoring and with a nod to styles and silhouettes from Sex, Pirate, and Mini-Crini collections.

LEFT: On the catwalk at Berlin Fashion Week in 2008, a model wears the Anglomania label.

OPPOSITE:
Vivienne Westwood Anglomania at Paris Fashion Days at Palais Brongniart in 2010.

Andreas Kronthaler for Vivienne Westwood

In 2016, what was formerly the Gold Label became Andreas Kronthaler for Vivienne Westwood. Kronthaler had been designing with Westwood for over 25 years and the change in name was an acknowledgement of this, though the pair would still be working together in the creation of the collections, which would not change so dramatically in style other than they perhaps felt a little lighter. Though subject matter regarding the environment would remain as prevalent and serious as ever.

In his first collection for autumn/winter 2016-17, titled Sexercise, Kronthaler made it a little more personal and referenced his Austrian heritage. Europa came next, for spring/summer 2017, and was dedicated to Europe – raffia dresses and neutral tones featured, and a particularly memorable piece was a dress that mimicked the naked female body. A&V followed for autumn/winter 2017-18 with Vivienne modelling, while Andreas was the title of his spring/summer 2018 collection – a personal exploration. Vivienne was the name of his autumn/winter 2018-19 collection and, as the name suggests, it was inspired by her.

OK... It's Showtime for spring/summer 2019, 7 for autumn/winter 2019-20, Rock Me Amadeus for spring/summer 2020, and Down to No.10 are among his other collections for the house since it became Andreas Kronthaler for Vivienne Westwood.

OPPOSITE:
A Vivienne Westwood magazine advert from the 2010s. The Andreas Kronthaler for Vivienne Westwood name would become official in 2016.

Muse, Sara Stockbridge

S ara Stockbridge, model, actress, musician and now writer, was muse to Vivienne Westwood throughout most of the 1980s and 1990s, walking in shows and featuring in campaigns. Her debut was in the Mini-Crini collection for spring/summer 1986 and she would often close shows as the Vivienne Westwood bride, a prized role for any model.

Her knowing eyes and cheeky grin encapsulated the wit and charm of the Westwood woman. She was also involved in Westwood's music project, called Choice – a band with Stockbridge as the lead singer. Since she stopped modelling, Stockbridge has appeared in Eastenders and The Glam Metal Detectives, among other shows, and released a couple of books. Following Jordan's early ambassador duties, it felt like Sara had taken on the mantle, until the supermodels became a common line-up at Westwood shows.

LEFT: Sara Stockbridge looking bridal for Vivienne Westwood during London Fashion Week 1993.

OPPOSITE: Muse Sara Stockbridge models Vivienne Westwood circa 1988.

Supermodel Moments

Courting attention has long been a speciality for Westwood – both in and out of fashion. But in the earlier days of the Vivienne Westwood brand, this was especially true on the catwalk. Mostly, it was because the clothes, with their eccentrically successful references plucked from the past, did the talking, and some instances the not-quite-so-walking. But other times, it was because of who was wearing the clothes. The 1980s and 1990s were the heyday of supermodels, and Westwood had her fair share of them on her catwalks. Kate Moss and Naomi Campbell

were regulars, as was Yasmin Le Bon and Helena Christensen. And there was also a future First Lady in Carla Bruni, who walked during the mid 1990s in a bikini and coat ensemble.

OPPOSITE: Model Carla Bruni at the Vivienne Westwood show in Paris circa 1994.

LEFT: Model Kristen McMenamy on the catwalk at the Vivienne Westwood spring/summer 1996 show in Paris, France.

Naomi Campbell's Platforms

It is a moment that has gone down in fashion history. The supermodel Naomi Campbell was a good sport when she fell from a pair of blue mock-croc platforms, the cult Super Elevated Gillie style, during the Anglomania show in 1993. Ever the professional, she was all smiles and giggles as she sat in the middle of the catwalk, having toppled from the towering shoes. The moment, and images of it, have become legendary. Had it happened during one of today's fashion weeks, ensconced as they are in the social media age, it would have gone viral.

Side note: it has been observed by Ian Kelly, Westwood's co-biographer, that shoe rehearsals are commonplace in preparation for couture shows – where collections often feature footwear as out of this world as the clothes that accompany them – but that they are of particular significance at Vivienne Westwood. On this occasion, it's easy to see why. Despite Campbell's fall, platforms have never stopped being a part of the Westwood repertoire, and Westwood herself often wore them.

RIGHT: Vivienne Westwood and Naomi Campbell at the 13th Annual Night of Stars at the Pierre Hotel, New York City in 1996.

OPPOSITE: The iconic Naomi Campbell moment.

Kate Moss' Accessories

At Paris Fashion Week for the spring/summer 1994 Cafe Society show, Kate Moss walked down the runway wearing a tiny skirt that sat on her hips, an orb necklace, pink buckled-up platforms and a Napolean-esque hat. One arm covered her topless bare chest and another held what appeared to be a Magnum ice cream that she was eating. It made for an eye-catching, and rather surprising, accessory. For the Vive La Cocotte collection for autumn/winter 1995-96, Moss seemed to swap the ice cream for a rabbit, walking the runway with a little ball of white fluff perched in her arms.

The Café Society collection was inspired, aptly, by the cafe society of 19th century Paris and was also an homage to the work of English couturier Charles Frederick Worth. Neat, structured and slim silhouettes featured alongside barely-there ensembles of short, short length.

OPPOSITE: Kate Moss appears to be holding a rabbit at the autumn/winter 1995-96 show.

LEFT: Kate Moss' iconic outfit at the spring/summer 1994 Vivienne Westwood catwalk show, Paris.

Pamela Anderson

Westwood and Pamela Anderson, the actress best-known for her role in 1990s beach-set television show Baywatch, had bonded over their interest in eco-political causes. Anderson, much like Westwood, had turned her attention to activism and campaigning for the climate, and in one another they found great allies. But their friendship extended beyond that. In 2009, Anderson modelled Westwood's autumn/winter 2009-10 Gold Label in Paris. This could have been foreseen, if one had been watching closely – Anderson had been spotted attending a previous Red Label show in London, causing quite the media frenzy.

The autumn/winter 2009-10 collection was titled +5° and in it Anderson wore a bright orange draped dress with lilac tulle wings splaying from the sides. Anderson would continue to play a role in the Westwood brand, featuring in future campaigns, wearing the pieces and sharing information regarding causes dear to her.

LEFT: Friend and fellow activist Pamela Anderson walks at the autumn/winter 2009 show in Paris.

OPPOSITE: Pamela Anderson and Westwood backstage at the Red Label spring/summer 2009 show at London Fashion Week.

Expansion Part Two

The 1990s was a time of expansion for the Vivienne Westwood brand. Collections were impactful, eyebrow-raising and influential. New diffusion lines were being introduced, as were new design ideas and reference points. And stores beyond the original Worlds End outpost were also on the horizon.

In 1990, the Davis Street boutique opened in London's Mayfair and later on that decade a boutique opened at 43 Conduit Street. It was in 1999 that the Vivienne Westwood New York store opened on Greene Street. Licensed boutiques also opened in Tokyo, Japan. And as the new millennium dawned, in 2001, the Vivienne Westwood e-commerce site debuted. The following year, stores opened in South Korea and Hong Kong, with a flagship in Japan in 2003, and another in Milan. There would also be New York and Paris flagships. It was a case of from King's Road to the rest of the world.

OPPOSITE: Red Label autumn/winter 1999 show in Manhattan.

ABOVE: Westwood in her SOHO boutique, New York, 1998.

Fragrance

What does Vivienne Westwood, the brand, smell like? It's an interesting question given the breadth of the designer's work and the varied nature of her cultural influences, both past and present.

It was in 1998 that a Vivienne Westwood fragrance made its debut. It was called Boudoir and, as *WWD* reported, was developed in conjunction with the famous "nose" (perfume artist, or perfumer) Martin Gras of Dragoco, a fragrance and flavour company, under a licensing deal with Lancaster.

Exuding a warm, spicy and floral aroma, the idea behind the name of the scent was that a boudoir, or a dressing room, is a signifier of a woman's space. In her boudoir, a woman can see her flaws as well as her potential – essentially she can be with herself on her own terms. The design of the bottle was also carefully considered. Inspired by antique perfume flacons, it featured a gold seal embossed with the orb logo. It was designed by Fabrice Legros.

OPPOSITE:
An advert for Boudoir
by Vivienne Westwood
in the 2000s.

BOUDOIR

Victoria & Albert Museum Exhibition

In 2004, the Victoria & Albert Museum held a landmark exhibition charting Westwood's contribution to fashion, the biggest dedicated to a British designer at the time. Running from April 1 to July 11 that year, it chronicled her work from punk through to the present day, with everything from sweeping ball gowns in strong, historical styles and those towering platforms that took Naomi Campbell down to a T-shirt worn by Johnny Rotten of the Sex Pistols among the sartorial journey on display. It was widely praised for its wow factor.

The Victoria & Albert Museum has various Westwood pieces among its collections. On display in its core fashion section is a look from the Seditionaries phase, which is housed in a section titled Deconstructing Fashion, cited as running from 1975 to 1985 when Japanese designers were also exploring what could and would outrage in fashion (the Japanese designers opted for the complete opposite of Westwood in all-black looks). Meanwhile, items from Westwood's most creative periods – Pirates, Buffalo Girls, Witches – are also among their archive collection, which is available to see online: it includes boots, corsets, slogan Ts and more.

The V&A retrospective is not the only time Westwood's work has been celebrated. In 2000, the Museum of London held the exhibition, Vivienne Westwood: the collection of

Romilly McAlpine.

And, in 2013, the Metropolitan Museum of Art in New York (often referred to as The Met) opened its annual fashion exhibition, Chaos to Couture, in which over 20 pieces of Westwood's work from the 1970s onwards were on show. The aim of the exhibition was to look at punk's influence on fashion throughout history and, arguably, among all the contributors to the show, Westwood was most relevant – certainly on the British side of things.

ABOVE: Vivienne Westwood at the press day for the VIVIENNE WESTWOOD 34 Years in Fashion exhibition in 2004 at the V&A in London.

OVERLEAF: Westwood among her designs at the launch of the exhibition Vivienne Westwood in Milan, 2007.

Awards and Accolades

The Vivienne Westwood mix of everything from punk to couture is a potent one, and would earn her many seals of approval throughout her career. A constant pioneer, a constant provocateur, she boasts an impressive list of awards and accolades to match. In 1990, and then again in 1991, she was awarded Fashion Designer of the Year by the British Fashion Council, which is the organisation that works to promote UK fashion globally. In 1992, she was made an Honorary Senior Fellow of the Royal College of Art. She won the inaugural Institute of Contemporary Arts Award for

Outstanding Contribution to Contemporary Culture in 1994; and in 1998 Vivienne Westwood Limited was awarded the Queen's Export Award.

In 2007, she was awarded Outstanding Achievement in Fashion at the British Fashion Awards in London and, the following year, received a Distinction from the Royal College of Art for her service to fashion.

In 2015, she received a Lifetime Achievement Award

from the Savannah College of Art & Design Museum of Arts. And in 2018, Vivienne Westwood was honoured with the Swarovski Award for Positive Change at The Fashion Awards (formerly the British Fashion Awards). The accolade came in recognition of her contribution to the fashion industry, as well as her work in engaging the industry in global change, plus her campaigning for Greenpeace's Save The Arctic, and Cool Earth's mission to save the rainforest.

A press release issued by the British Fashion Council at the time quoted Caroline Rush, the Chief Executive, as saying: "With this special award, Dame Vivienne Westwood will be recognised for being a campaigner for change throughout her career. She has led the way championing humanitarian and environmental issues, and her contribution to British fashion makes her one of the most respected designers in the fashion industry and a great inspiration to us all. Her most recent campaign has led more businesses in the fashion industry in the UK to 'Switch to Green Energy' and she continues to inspire many more to do the same." To receive her award, she wore an A-line dress with braces and jacket from the Andreas Kronthaler for Vivienne Westwood autumn/winter 2018-19 collection. Accompanying her to the awards, Kronthaler wore a Vivienne Westwood tailored suit with a coat from the Vivienne Westwood x Burberry collaboration collection – a clever pairing that could also be deemed something of an accolade.

OPPOSITE: Westwood and Kronthaler at the Fashion Awards at Royal Albert Hall, London, December 10, 2018.

ABOVE: Westwood in her Camden Town Studio, 1990, apparently taken after she won another award.

Receiving her OBE

Westwood is famous for many things, but among her own personal accolades is the time she received her OBE from Queen Elizabeth II at Buckingham Palace in 1992. As fashion moments go, this has to be right up there. Although it was no accident that Westwood was being bestowed with such an honour, what happened while she was being photographed was completely unplanned. As she twirled in her grey skirt suit to pose for photographers after the ceremony (the circle skirt was from the Grand Hotel collection), she exposed her bare crotch. In something of a fashion urban myth, she claimed that the Queen found it amusing. Regardless, Westwood going commando to collect her OBE was seen as being very punk indeed. Later, in 2006, she was made Dame Commander of the Order of the British Empire and received it from Prince Charles, a member of the Royal Family she has said she was a fan of.

OPPOSITE: Westwood at Buckingham Palace after receiving her OBE from the Queen.

LEFT: Westwood posing for photographers after collecting her ensignia from the Prince of Wales at Buckingham Palace.

Here Comes the Bride

In 1992, Westwood introduced wedding gowns to her spring/summer range. It might have seemed like an unexpected move for the original queen of anti-establishment but, over the years, Westwood's cultural horizons and inspirations had expanded to include more elaborate, aristocratic and regal realms with pomp and splendour – couture. Seasonal collections shown in Paris featuring corsets and lavish gowns would have been entirely suited to a wedding, whether they were meant to be or not.

Bridal has since grown into its own very successful line, with designs available from dedicated stores, as well as the renowned Browns Bride in London. Styles are signature but classic Westwood, and include the corsets for which the brand is so well-known, full sweeping skirts, draped necklines and that strong sense of history reinvented, pertinently, for the modern bride. Lucky brides including Dita Von Teese, the fictional Carrie Bradshaw, Miley Cyrus, Lorraine Pascale and even Miss Piggy have all enjoyed a Westwood wedding moment.

Dita Von Teese wore a spectacular purple gown for her wedding to the musician Marilyn Manson in 2005. And WikiLeaks founder Julian Assange and his wife were also wed in Westwood. Miss Piggy, meanwhile, the diva of Jim Henson's The Muppets, hired Westwood to design her wedding gown – even though her beloved frog companion, Kermit, had yet to propose. The ivory-coloured couture gown was decorated with paillettes made using recycled plastic bottles and featured in the *Muppets Most Wanted* film in 2014. Quite brilliantly, it didn't stop there. Westwood designed other outfits for Miss Piggy in the film as well – they included a Harris Tweed hound's tooth check coat and matching beret, plus a silver hand-embroidered floral lace gown. How could Kermit possibly have refused? More recently, Bella Hadid became the bride at the end of the autumn/winter 2020-21 show: she wore a sheer white lace wedding dress.

LEFT:
Model Bella Hadid does bridal at the Vivienne Westwood autumn/winter 2020-21 show at Paris Fashion Week.

OVERLEAF: From *Muppets Most Wanted*, Miss Piggy in a wedding gown designed by Vivienne Westwood, 2014.

Sex and the City

In the 2008 film version of the acclaimed television series *Sex and the City*, Carrie Bradshaw (played by Sarah Jessica Parker) wears Vivienne Westwood on what is surely one of the most important days of her fashionista-columnist's life: her wedding. Sadly, she doesn't actually get around to getting married in it, but the dress has since gone down in fashion history. Said dress is the Cloud wedding gown from the autumn/winter 2007-8 collection, titled Wake Up, Cave Girl, which comprises an angular Wilma corset in gold-backed ivory and silk duchesse satin with a crushed skirt in ivory silk Radzimir taffeta.

According to Westwood's own biography, written with Ian Kelly, Anna Wintour had suggested the American designer Vera Wang to the producers, but Parker had personally insisted on wearing a dress by Westwood and as filming got underway the voluminous cloud dress was redesigned by Westwood specifically for the Carrie Bradshaw character.

OPPOSITE: Actresses Sarah Jessica Parker, Kristin Davis, Kim Cattral and Cynthia Nixon on the set of *Sex and the City: The Movie* on location on the Upper East Side in New York City in 2007. Parker is wearing the Vivienne Westwood Cloud wedding gown.

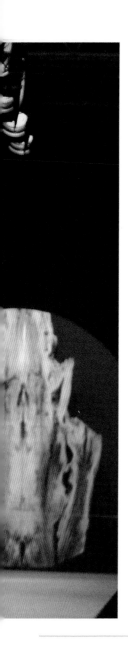

Bradshaw initially opts for a vintage skirt suit, but upon wearing the Westwood gown for a Vogue shoot in the film, is gifted the dress by the designer – who, incidentally, did actually write the handwritten note that accompanied it in the film. Its exaggerated silhouette features a nipped-in waist and it is quite the show-stopping gown. Bradshaw wore it with a feather in her hair for the film. Ten years after the film's release, Westwood created a series of ready-to-wear pieces inspired by that very dress: the Wilma cocktail dress in three different styles, and the Wilma corset, available in black and red.

More recently, the dress has been back in action for filming of the second season of the *Sex And The City* spinoff *And Just Like That*. Sarah Jessica Parker has been seen wearing the Westwood wedding gown with a turquoise cape-and-gloves, and matching feather in her hair. As a result of this dress being featured in the original film, Westwood's profile increased in America.

OPPOSITE: Carrie's *Sex and the City* wedding dress on the runway at the Vivienne Westwood autumn/winter 2007-08 collection during Paris Fashion Week.

On the Red Carpet

Owing to their drama and grandeur, which warmly invite the wearer to strike a pose, Westwood's designs can frequently be seen on the red carpet at premieres and award ceremonies. At the 95th Academy Awards, held in March 2023, the actress Elizabeth Banks was among those who wore a bespoke Vivienne Westwood gown, which featured a train at the back. Oscar nominee (for *Sense & Sensibility*) Kate Winslet wore a pink Vivienne Westwood gown with a contrasting wrap in 1996 which, according to VanityFair. com, had been made especially for her. It featured a scoop neck and was worn with an Edwardian diamond necklace from Martin Katz.

Other well-known names who are fans, friends and wearers of the brand include Gwen Stefani, Helena Bonham Carter (who gave a speech at the late designer's memorial about how great her creations were), Sarah Jessica Parker, Rihanna, Zendaya, Blake Lively, Elle Fanning, Kim Kardashian, Dua Lipa, Christina Ricci (who wore a tartan mini dress to The Met Gala for the Punk: Chaos to Couture exhibit), Thandiwe Newton, Nigella Lawson, Lily Cole, Tracey Emin, Helen Mirren, Christina Hendricks, Pamela Anderson, as well as Bradley Cooper and Matthew McConaughey.

Such has been the brand's success on the red carpet that in 2014, a Red Carpet capsule was introduced, reported *WWD*, which drew inspiration from the English couturier Charles Frederick Worth with elaborate silhouettes. Among them was

the bustier-style Melba dress, and the Dora style constructed from drapes and folds.

And it will forever be in the history books now: singer Katy Perry wore the brand to the coronation of King Charles III. At the ceremony itself, she wore a bespoke lilac short-sleeved jacket and a matching skirt, while at the Coronation Concert she wore a bespoke gold corseted gown with draped sleeves.

ABOVE: Actress Elle Fanning at the *Ishmael's Ghosts* screening and Opening Gala during the 70th annual Cannes Film Festival in 2017.

Campaigns

B esides Westwood's political campaigns, there are the
Vivienne Westwood fashion campaigns, for the seasonal
collections. Often photographed by Juergen Teller, who
has been a long-time collaborator, they are instantly
recognisable for his raw style, which works well with the
typically bright colours, bold silhouettes and off-kilter or
madcap mood of a Westwood/Kronthaler collection.

In 2008 Pamela Anderson became the face of the brand. The
spring/summer 2009 campaign was shot at her Miami trailer
and she featured in two more campaigns, including Andreas
Kronthaler for Vivienne Westwood spring/summer 2017.

Westwood has also featured in the brand's campaigns –
notably, during the global pandemic and lockdown. At this
time, many brands – including high street brands – had to
pivot and think outside the box to come up with creative
ideas and imagery to promote their upcoming collections.
For autumn/winter 2021, Andreas Kronthaler for Vivienne
Westwood starred Westwood dressed up in the collection,
posing around the Battersea studio, rolls of vibrant fabric
behind and around her. Kronthaler was the master behind
the lens this time around, though he would next join
Westwood as a campaign lead in the spring/summer 2022
campaign photographed in Naples once again by Teller.

OPPOSITE: Westwood and longtime collaborator Juergen Teller at a private view
of his exhibition Demelza Kids at Bonhams in 2019 in London.

RIP 40 Years of Punk

In November 2016 Joe Corré, the son of Vivienne Westwood and Malcolm McLaren, set fire to an estimated £5 m worth of punk memorabilia on a boat on the river Thames. He did so on what was supposed to be the 40th anniversary of anarchy – when the Sex Pistols had launched their song 'Anarchy in the UK'. His motive, he told press at the time, was that punk was not meant to be nostalgic. And he didn't think it was something you could learn to be, buy into or recreate. It was reported that he wasn't impressed by plans to celebrate the 40th anniversary of the style and music subculture in London via a series of cultural events, which he felt went against the very idea of it in the first place.

Effigies of politicians, as well as the items such as clothes, posters and memorabilia were loaded with fireworks and set alight near Albert Bridge in Chelsea. Westwood watched from the bank of the river among a crowd of onlookers, and took the opportunity to promote her green message from the top of a green double decker bus. This flashy act of rebellion was met with a mixed response, with some not deeming it a very punk thing to do at all.

Documenting Westwood

It's no secret that Westwood has been the documentor of many a fashion moment and movement, and more recently of global concerns and issues regarding climate change or politics. She has also been the subject of numerous books and films herself (and from time to time has even featured in her own campaigns), which, as one of British fashion's most significant protagonists, makes sense.

In 2014, for the first time and in collaboration with the author Ian Kelly, Westwood released a personal memoir, simply called *Vivienne Westwood*, that charted her life from childhood to the latest show she was working on, with details of the fashion industry, the business, her collections, friends and collaborators all included.

Alongside her husband, she featured in a short film called *Trouble in Paradise* in 2015. The couple play Adam and Eve and encounter the fall of humankind. Westwood also plays a judge who finds humankind guilty of ecocide. It is both surreal and slightly haunting – one imagines, the latter is deliberate.

In 2016, she released *Get A Life: The Diaries of Vivienne Westwood*, which was based on her online diary that she had begun in 2010. In it, she covered what she was up to in a few entries each month – be that heading to the rainforest or to David Cameron's house in the Cotswolds (with a tank, no less).

The specifics of her collections were brought together in *Vivienne Westwood Catwalk*, a celebration of 40 years, which also coincided with her 80th birthday. Bound in the Westwood MacAndreas tartan and printed on FSC (Forest Stewardship Council) paper, it features 1300 looks from over 70 collections, as they originally appeared.

ABOVE: Westwood at an event held in St James' Church, London, for her new book *Get A Life! The Diaries of Vivienne Westwood* in 2016.

A Film By LORNA TUCKER

WESTWOOD

Punk. Icon. Activist.

In 2018, the filmmaker Lorna Tucker took her film *Westwood: Punk, Icon, Activist* to the Sundance Film Festival. It featured archive and current footage, with interviews among her inner circle. The aim was to portray Westwood as a designer and activist, but Westwood seems to have been unhappy with the result and the brand issued a statement on Twitter distancing themselves from the project. It seems that Westwood felt it didn't convey enough activism and featured footage and content that was already readily available.

Meanwhile, *Wake Up Punk*, a documentary film released in May 2022, was geared towards telling the story of why Joe Corré, Westwood's son with Malcolm McLaren, chose to destroy what was reportedly £5 million worth of punk memorabilia, with insights from Westwood on punk along the way.

And, more recently, as part of London Craft Week in May 2023, the Vivienne Westwood flagship Conduit Street store in Mayfair paid homage to a Vivienne Westwood icon, the corset – which had started to feature prevalently in collections during the 1980s. Vivienne Westwood Corsets: 1987–Present Day featured key archive and show pieces. The aim was to explore the fashion house's approach to underwear as outerwear in terms of historical dress, culture and fine art.

OPPOSITE: A poster for the documentary *Westwood: Punk, Icon, Activist*, 2018.

Climate Activism

During her lifetime, Westwood was an avid supporter of, and involved with, various NGOs, charities and causes. These included: Reprieve, Liberty, Amnesty International, The Refugee Council, PETA, The Environmental Justice Foundation and Friends of the Earth. Also important to her were the plights of Leonard Peltier, Chelsea Manning and Julian Assange. She also backed Greenpeace's Save the Arctic Campaign, and the rainforest charity Cool Earth.

It was during the mid-noughties that her fashion started to morph into activism – in some ways a reprise of her punk roots geared towards modern concerns. She had read an article by the environmentalist and scientist James Lovelock that inspired her to write her own 'Active Resistance to Propaganda' manifesto. It featured her own thoughts and a kind of agenda on how to save the environment; and encouraged the idea of buying less, choosing well and making things last. It was the beginning of her own Climate Revolution, which would get its own grand reveal at the closing ceremony of the London Paralympics where she managed to reveal a cape with Climate Revolution written across it for all to see. She also introduced a blog for it, in which her thoughts and ideas could be read alongside her correspondence to, for example, Julian Assange, whom she had been a staunch supporter of. There is also a YouTube channel.

OPPOSITE: Westwood promotes her Climate Revolution at London Fashion Week, where she presented her spring/summer 2013 Red Label collection.

Westwood would visit the rainforest via NGO Cool Earth, having met Matthew Owen, its director, in 2010. It became a growing concern of hers and she donated £1 million to them, and thereafter drew attention to the cause in collections and interviews – memorably, in one Jonathan Ross interview, she hardly spoke about clothes at all. Reportedly, it won her a fan in Prince Charles, who is known for his environmental work.

It is also through her climate activism work that she met Pamela Anderson who, originally invited to one of her shows, realised she was more interested in her eco-credentials and the manifesto.

Westwood would travel to Africa for the first time in 2011, for the International Trade Centre of the United

Nations, and set up a scheme to help employ women, producing bags and handcrafted items that would sell under the Vivienne Westwood label using recycled materials. Ever since, the brand has aspired to use collections, collaborations and the catwalk to promote awareness and campaign for a better world. Today, the website acknowledges that this is something of a contradiction – to promote sustainability activism but be in fashion, which is about producing and buying to set cycles. The website also points out the ways in which the brand plans to combat this: from reducing the size of collections and using leftover stock to finding alternatives to conventional materials and travelling by the greenest methods possible when it's unavoidable.

OPPOSITE: Westwood at the People's March for Climate, Justice and Jobs on Park Lane, London, in 2015.

In 2017, the brand teamed up with the British Fashion Council and the Mayor of London to encourage the fashion industry to switch to a renewable energy supplier or tariff.

Westwood also supported the Save The Arctic campaign in the early 00s, which played out at London Waterloo Station via a series of celebrity portraits photographed by Andy Gotts MBE. Each celebrity wore a Vivienne Westwood Save The Arctic organic cotton T-shirt and all profits went to Greenpeace. Notable faces included Hugh Grant, George Clooney, Kate Moss, Sarah Ferguson and Julian Assange.

During the mid 00s, Westwood's collections began to centre on social justice and political causes. Autumn/winter 2005-6's Propaganda also marked a move towards what would be a prevailing influence from now on: the environment. Chaos Point for autumn/winter 2008-9, Do It Yourself for spring/summer 2009, +5 degrees for autumn/winter 2009-10 (in which Pamela Anderson walked), Get A Life for spring/summer 2010, Gaia The Only One for spring/summer 2011, War & Peace for spring/summer 2012, Climate Revolution for spring/summer 2013, Save The Arctic for autumn/winter 2013-14, Everything is Connected for spring/summer 2014, Save the Rainforest for autumn/winter 2014-15, End Ecocide for spring/summer 2015, Mirror The World

for spring/summer 2016 and Down to No.10 for spring/
summer 2021 all had the rainforest, ecology and saving the
environment as key messages. To close her Red Label show for
the spring/summer 2013 season, she wore a pair of hotpants,
tights and a T-shirt calling for Climate Revolution.

Protest

P rotest is in Westwood's DNA as much as tartan and
pearls, and in many ways her work with climate change
has taken her on a full-circle moment back to punk. She
was against capitalism and the government but for the
environment and human rights. As such, her catwalks have
often been used as the stomping ground on which to promote
her politics – models carrying placards reading "Climate
Revolution" and "Austerity is a Crime" among them. There
have also been flash mobs out on the streets at fashion week.
Where there was a will, there was certainly a Westwood way.

It's what saw her and McLaren have a few run-ins with the
law early on in her career and it's what prompted her to come
up with even more bodacious stunts in recent years to get her
message across, taking big actions to make big points.

What must Prime Minister David Cameron have thought
when Vivienne Westwood turned up to his constituency
home in a tank to protest fracking in 2015? It turns out he
was in Leeds at the time. But, sat atop the vehicle, she went
into a proverbial battle, driving through Oxfordshire to carry
out her own "attack" in response to a previous announcement
from the government that it would offer licenses for fracking
in various locations, the Guardian reported.

OPPOSITE: In July 2020, Westwood was harnessed into a giant birdcage and
suspended 10 feet in the air in front of the Old Bailey Criminal Court in protest
about the US extradition trial of Julian Assange.

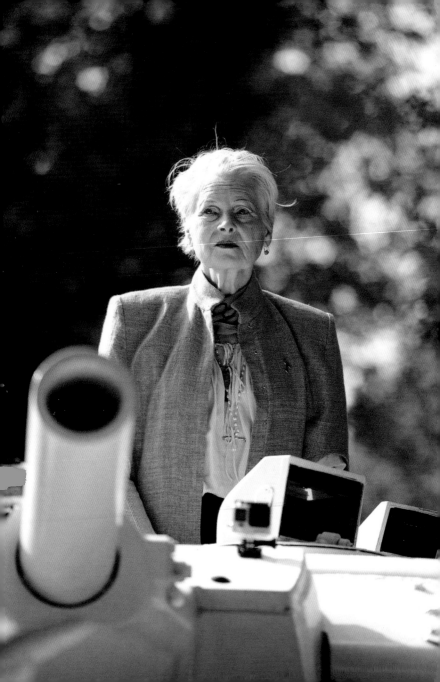

The designer condemned the controversial technique used to extract gas from beneath the ground, a subject she has long been outspoken on. A quick Google of Westwood and the word fracking will bring up pages of stories and images of her leading the charge on the issue.

Whether this incident was as attention-grabbing as her 2020 birdcage stunt is up for debate. Westwood once again made the headlines when she suspended herself in a giant birdcage outside the Old Bailey Criminal Court, dressed in a bright yellow suit and black combat boots. Speaking through a megaphone, she expressed her support once more for the WikiLeaks founder Julian Assange, and had an "I'm Julian Assange" poster on the cage. She had been creating T-shirts with the same slogan and an image of her face since 2012, in support of him.

But, even before all of this, there was a memorable *Tatler* cover in 1989 featuring Westwood dressed up as Margaret Thatcher, and the likeness is uncanny. Politicians are one thing Westwood was very much against.

Westwood was never afraid to step into the limelight and protest in the name of a cause, as she did with her "I am not a terrorist" T-shirts in 2005, and the "Yes" badges in reference to supporting Scottish independence. It was due to the fact that she was at another protest – the strikes in the UK in 2022 – that Westwood was absent from the last Andreas Kronthaler for Vivienne Westwood show before her death.

OPPOSITE: Taking aim, Dame Vivienne Westwood protests anti-fracking in a tank on the way to the constituency home of Prime Minister David Cameron, in Witney, Oxfordshire.

Vivienne Westwood
x Burberry

For the past 20 years, fashion has loved nothing better than a collaboration. And, over the past decade, there have been an abundance of them, from the mixing of high street brands with high fashion brands to designer names teaming up with fellow designer names. Step forward Vivienne Westwood x Burberry – which came a good few years before Balenciaga's Gucci Hack and the Versace x Fendi Fendace swap.

It was in July 2018 that the British brand Burberry – which is known for its checks and craftsmanship – announced a collaboration with Vivienne Westwood via Instagram, with a picture of the designer, Andreas Kronthaler and the Burberry creative director Riccardo Tisci. It was an ideal match: both are British brands, and both pay homage to the craft and history of clothes. Harris Tweed and tartan have been signatures of Westwood while checked cloth is a lynchpin of Burberry.

Later that year, following the announcement, the two brands started to reveal what the limited edition collection of the re-imagined pieces would look like. It included a mini kilt as well as lace-up platforms in Burberry's vintage check, while a new logo combined both brand names together with Burberry in black and Vivienne Westwood in red.

The collection released with a campaign by photographer

David Sims, which was shot in London and featured Kate Moss as well as Sistren, Leonard Emmanuel, LadyFag, DelaRosa, Josh Quinton, Andy Bradin, Claudia Lavender, Marco Motta, Sashadavai and Jacob Shifrin, who all modelled the unisex pieces. Westwood and Kronthaler also appeared in the campaign, which featured double-breasted and hugger jackets. A T-shirt with a Westwood message hand-written on it went towards supporting the rainforest charity Cool Earth. Prices began at a very reasonable £55.

While this was something of a blockbuster of a collaboration, there had been other Westwood x fashion brand collaborations prior to this: Eastpak, Asics, Vans and Melissa shoes. The French footwear brand worked with Vivienne Westwood Anglomania to create a cult take on the traditional jelly shoe in 2009. In bold colours, it featured a heart-shaped toe in what could have been thought of as a reworking of the iconic – and divisive – animal toe shoes.

There have also been plenty of team-ups for cultural or charitable causes, with the English National Ballet, Virgin Atlantic and Red Nose Day. Westwood's biggest collaborations have undoubtedly come by way of her activism and protest work.

LEFT: The then-Burberry creative director Riccardo Tisci - with whom Westwood collaborated - takes a bow at the Burberry spring/summer 2020 fashion show at London Fashion Week in 2019.

The TikTok Necklace Phenomenon

In 2021, Westwood's Bas Relief pearl choker had a moment with Gen Z. And it was all down to the popular social media platform TikTok, where influencers and celebrities alike had rediscovered it – and were wearing it so much that a trend forecaster termed it the "TikTok necklace" in an article by *The New York Times*, which charted its rise and original provenance. It would simply be known as the TikTok necklace thereafter.

Pearls have long had a place in the Vivienne Westwood woman's wardrobe, first appearing among her Harris Tweed collection before this specific necklace design made its appearance in the 1990 Portrait collection. Priced at £400, it features three rows of hand-knotted Swarovski pearls that fasten with a branded closure at the back, while a bold orb sits at the front. Among its celebrity fans include Kylie Jenner, Bella Hadid, Dua Lipa and Rihanna. Such was its success that for the spring/summer 2022 season, the brand put out an updated version of the choker-style necklace.

OPPOSITE: Singer Dua Lipa attends
The BRIT Awards 2021 at the O2
Arena London on May 11, 2021,
wearing the TikTok pearl necklace
by Vivienne Westwood.

The Last Show

Though collections, since 2016, had been known as Andreas Kronthaler for Vivienne Westwood, the pair would often still take a bow together. It was always a collaborative creative process between them. Kronthaler's last collection before Westwood's death was for the spring/summer 2023 season, shown in Paris in October 2022. He had been inspired by a book he was reading, *Super-Infinite: The Transformations of John Dunne* by Katherine Rundell, which translated into a sexy take on Renaissance themes for a collection full of very high platforms and slinky knitwear, plus flashy patent and punches of red.

Georgia May Jagger walked. And, reportedly, one of the models did fall from their lofty heights. But on this occasion, Kronthaler would be taking the bow by himself – in typical Westwood fashion, the designer had stayed behind in London to join in the national day of strikes and protest.

OPPOSITE: Andreas Kronthaler with the models Stella Maxwell, Bella Hadid and Irina Shayk on the runway at the Vivienne Westwood spring/summer 2023 show during Paris Fashion Week.

A Punk Pioneer

Vivienne Westwood, iconoclast and activist, died on December 29, 2022, at the age of 81. It was announced via the brand's Instagram and was reported that she had died peacefully at home in Clapham with her family. She had apparently been designing up until the last moment. Her husband, Kronthaler, said she had left him with lots to be getting on with. Following the news, an outpouring of tributes came from the fashion industry, as well as from fans and passers-by of the Worlds End store on King's Road, whose exterior now had flowers and letters laid outside in tribute.

Not long after her passing, news broke that Paco Rabanne, the Spanish-French fashion designer who had innovated a space age style, had also died. It felt like the end of an era: of the great designers who defined eras, and invented the future of fashion.

It was observed by fashion commentators that Westwood's spirit lived on through a handful of London fashion designers at the London Fashion Week season, in February 2023 – Matty Bovan and Harris Reed among them. And London Fashion Week was dedicated to the queen of punk, queen of couture, queen of controversy, Dame Vivienne Westwood.

OPPOSITE: January 2023, tributes are made to the late Dame Vivienne Westwood outside the legendary King's Road shop in Chelsea.

LFW Memorial Service

London Fashion Week February 2023 was, as the British Fashion Council announced, dedicated to Vivienne Westwood. It was during the biannual trade showcase that a memorial was held for Dame Vivienne Westwood, a much-loved and celebrated character who had also shown her Red Label in the capital on numerous occasions throughout her career. It took place at Southwark Cathedral on February 16.

As one would imagine, it was attended by the great and good of fashion, many of whom were dressed in her designs, sporting tartan, slogans, platforms or stylistic concoctions befitting the creator of fashion history, protest and activism. Among others, Kate Moss, Paul Smith, Victoria Beckham, Zandra Rhodes, Beth Ditto, Stormzy, Bianca Jagger, Tracey Emin, Pam Hogg, Richard E. Grant, Bobby Gillespie, Bob Geldof, Jonathan Ross, Sadie Frost, Will Young, Anna Wintour and Helena Bonham Carter turned out to say farewell to Westwood at a 90-minute memorial service. In it, Kronthaler shared stories of his life with Westwood and how they had met. A brass band local to Tintwistle also performed, as did Nick Cave and Chrissie Hynde. Her son Joseph also spoke and the actress Helena Bonham Carter shared her love for Westwood's clothes and thanked her for her dynamic knowledge in making them.

OPPOSITE: Actress, and fan of the brand, Helena Bonham Carter at the Vivienne Westwood memorial service at Southwark Cathedral in London.

Tintwistle

T he Andreas Kronthaler Vivienne Westwood autumn/
winter 2023-24 collection, which was shown in Paris
in the salons of Hôtel de la Marine in March 2023, was
the first show Kronthaler had done without his beloved
Vivienne. It had been less than three months since her
passing and for Kronthaler, naturally, it was an emotional
experience; as it was for audience members and critics who
noted at the time that it was hard to hold back the tears.

Kronthaler dedicated the show to Westwood and wrote
a touching and personal tribute to her as part of the
press notes, recalling pertinent moments in their creative
life together, which included the development of the
"masturbation skirt", designed for easy access, which he had
reprised once again. It was fittingly provocative.

Poignantly, the collection was titled Tintwistle, observing
the designer's place of birth, the village in Derbyshire where
she is also now buried. It also featured more reworked
Westwood hits: towering platforms that were reportedly
made even higher than the ones Naomi Campbell had
tumbled from some 20 years earlier (though on this
occasion, no one fell), little ruched skirts akin to the
original mini-crinis, boned corsets and pirate boots. There
were kilts, tartan and cocktail dresses. He had used antique
fabric that they had collected together and said that he
hoped she didn't mind. It was, of course, exactly the sort of
thing Westwood would have done herself, with her ongoing

mantra of buying less. His final sign-off mentioned her love for platforms and how she had always said it was important to put women on a pedestal.

As it came to a close Cora Corré, Westwood's granddaughter, became the bride in a micro-length wedding gown.

ABOVE: Andreas Kronthaler and Cora Corré at the end of the autum/winter 2023-24 show at Paris Fashion Week.

OVERLEAF: Cora Corré and Andreas Kronthaler backstage at the autumn/winter 2023-24 show, at Paris Fashion Week.

A Lasting Legacy

It's safe to say that today there isn't a fashion student who hasn't been inspired by Vivienne Westwood. To say that her impact on fashion and culture is significant is an understatement, whether you were a fan or not. She invented new things in fashion, which is rare. And from the very beginning she brought politics into fashion, later adding activism into the mix. She had fun but she was serious, too.

As a young fashion journalist I remember first interviewing Westwood in Paris before her Gold Label show. The interview ran late and she didn't answer a single question I asked. I'm not sure I was even able to get one in. No matter   accounts from other journalists are similar and we remember her fondly. She had more important things on her mind: her causes and her activism.

Cue the Vivienne Foundation, established in 2019 but launched at the beginning of 2023, which will upkeep these causes. It is a not-for-profit company founded by Westwood, her two sons and granddaughter and aims to preserve and continue the legacy of her life across design and activism, raising awareness and creating realistic change working with NGOs.

The foundation is built on four pillars: Climate Change,

OPPOSITE: Cora Corré, Dame Vivienne Westwood and Joe Corré pose backstage at the Vivienne Westwood show during London Fashion Week, January 2017.

Stop War, Defend Human Rights, Protest Capitalism. On the Climate Revolution website you will find the designer's musings on all of these topics, plus correspondence with those she supported.

LEFT: Westwood was
often seen cycling;
here, leaving
Scott's restaurant in
London in 2011.

Image Credits

Page 5 Ian Dickson/Contributor/Getty; 7 Victor VIRGILE/Contributor/Getty; 8 Peter Cade/Stringer/Getty; 9 John Stoddart/Popperfoto/Contributor/Getty; 11 dpa picture alliance/Alamy Stock Photo; 12-13 Graphic House/Staff/Getty; 14-15 Sueddeutsche Zeitung Photo/Alamy Stock Photo; 17 Mirrorpix/Contributor/Getty; 18 Express/Stringer/Getty; 19 David Montgomery/Contributor/Getty; 21 Erica Echenberg/Contributor/Getty; 22 Homer Sykes/Contributor/Getty; 23 Mirrorpix / Contributor / Getty; 25 Homer Sykes/Alamy Stock Photo/Alamy; 26 Michael Webb/Stringer/Getty; 27 Mirrorpix/Contributor/Getty; 28 Trinity Mirror/Mirrorpix/Alamy Stock Photo; 29 Ebet Roberts/Contributor/Getty; 30 Mirrorpix/Contributor/Getty; 31 Mirrorpix/Contributor/Getty; 32 Trinity Mirror/Mirrorpix/Alamy Stock Photo; 33 Trinity Mirror/Mirrorpix/Alamy Stock Photo; 34 PYMCA/Avalon/Contributor/Getty; 35 Mim Friday/Alamy Stock Photo; 37 Christopher Polk/Staff/Getty; 38 stockeurope/Alamy Stock Photo; 41 PA Images / Alamy Stock Photo; 42-43 Pascal Le Segretain/Staff/Getty; 44 Image Press/Contributor/Getty; 45 Dave Benett/Contributor/Getty; 46-47 John van Hasselt – Corbis/Contributor/Getty; 48 Denis O'Regan/Contributor/Getty; 49 WWD/Contributor/Getty; 50 David Corio/Contributor/Getty; 51 WWD/Contributor/Getty; 52 Dave Hogan/Contributor/Getty; 53 Dave Hogan/Contributor/Getty; 54 WWD/Contributor/Getty; 55 WWD/Contributor/Getty; 56 Bernard Weil/Contributor/

Getty; 57 John Stoddart/Popperfoto/Contributor/Getty; 59 Trinity Mirror/Mirrorpix/Alamy Stock Photo; 60 Dave Benett/Contributor/Getty; 61 Associated Press/Alamy Stock Photo; 62 John Stoddard/Popperfoto/Contributor/Getty; 63 Associated Press / Alamy Stock Photo; 64 DEUTSCH Jean-Claude/Contributor/Getty; 65 John van Hasselt – Corbis/Contributor/Getty; 66-67 Chris J Ratcliffe/Stringer/Getty; 68 PA Imags/Alamy Stock Photo; 69 Sipa USA/Alamy Stock Photo; 70 Ian Gavan/Stringer/Getty; 71 WWD Contributor/Getty; 72 Retro AdArchives/Alamy Stock Photo; 73 PA Images/Alamy Stock Photo; 75 Jon van Hasselt – Corbis/Contributor/Getty; 77 Jason LaVeris/Contributor/Getty; 78 Retro AdArchives/Alamy Stock Photo; 79 Pool ARNAL/GARCIA/Contributor/Getty; 80 PA Images/Alamy Stock Photo; 81 PA Images/Alamy Stock Photo; 82 Penske Media/Contributor; 83 dpa picture alliance archive/Alamy Stock Photo; 84 dpa picture alliance archive/Alamy Stock Photo; 85 Victor Boyko/Contributor/Getty; 86 Retro AdArchives/Alamy Stock Photo; 88 Mirrorpix/Contributor/Getty; 89 WWD/Contributor/Getty; 90 Michel Dufour/Contributor/Getty; 91 Images Press/Contributor/Getty; 92 Rose Hartman/Contributor/Getty; 93 PA Images/Alamy Stock Photo; 94 Daniel SIMON/Contributor/Getty; 95 Dave M. Benett/Contributor/Getty; 96 Antonio de Moraes Barros Filho/Contributor/Getty; 97 Mike Marsland/Contributor/Getty; 98 Penske Media/Contributor/Getty; 99 Rose Hartman/Contributor/Getty; 101 Retro AdArchives/Alamy Stock Photo; 103 Independent/Alamy Stock Photo; 104-105 Associated Press / Alamy Stock Phot; 106 UPI/Alamy Stock Photo; 107 Neil Turner/Alamy Stock Photo; 108 PA Images/Alamy Stock Photo; 109 AFP/Stringer/Getty; 111 Sipa US/Alamy Stock Photo; 112-113

RIGHT: The epitome of punk: Westwood with shop assistant Jordan and a friend in London, 1977.